HISTORY ISN'T BORING, YOUR TEACHER WAS

Mind Blowing Stories from American History in 90 Seconds or Less

KP Burke

ISBN: 979-8-218-52653-5

Cover design by: Karlie Sonne

For Mom, who encouraged me to read and write.

For Dad, who dragged us to all those forts and battlefields.

For Kerri, always the Tom Sawyer to my Huck Finn.

For Private First Class Martin Z. Boyajian (WW2), who showed me that heroes aren't just found in history books...sometimes they are also your Grandfather.

For Karlie, the one who keeps making my dreams come true everyday of our lives. I love you.

And

For Dan Sickles, the craziest bastard in U.S. History.

INTRODUCTION

Hi, I'm KP Burke and history isn't boring but hopefully this intro isn't either...

In December of 2023, I had a seizure and spent the two days before Christmas in the ICU at Morristown Hospital in NJ. I'm fine now but it scared the crap out of me. I had my girl (Karlie) and family with me and even the great Bobby Kelly called me to tell me he loved me (I should really call him back).

When you are awake with a breathing tube shoved down your throat, it gives you time to think. I told myself that the second I got out of there, I would release the three videos on Instagram that I had recorded weeks earlier.

The videos were a concept that my pal Mike Harrington at Gas Digital Network had come up with; take crazy stories from my podcast "American Loser" and break them down into 90 second clips.

Let me rewind that... so, "American Loser" is the podcast that I had started with my father, Larry Burke and we released more than 200 episodes, recording almost weekly for four years (it is still available wherever you listen to podcasts by the way). It picked up a solid and passionate listener base and we made some great friends along the way.

The concept was to take my idea for a book and instead (because I thought it would be easier), turn it into a podcast. The book idea was simple, I wanted to take John F. Kennedy's "Profiles in Courage" but use it to showcase the "Losers" from American history. The "Losers" were composed of complete scoundrels/dirtbags like Dan Sickles, others with hard luck stories that didn't get their moment in the spotlight, like Tesla and some with stories so insane, like Jack Parson's, we couldn't tell if what we were reading was true.

So, instead of a book, I created a podcast and enjoyed every moment of it working with my dad, where we essentially (and quite accidentally), wrote several books worth of "Losers" to prepare. Week in and week out we just kept writing because people were listening and enjoying it. It felt like total proof that if you are passionate about something, it can be contagious.

We recorded every episode at "A Shared Universe Podcast Studio" in Monmouth County, NJ. At that time, it was owned by Mike Zapcic and Ming Chen, both of "Comic Book Men" fame and friends I had made through the world of Kevin Smith (google, KP Burke - Brian O'Halloran Roast to see how this all accidentally came together).

After a phone call to Mike, we quickly booked our first session and met our sound guy. A timid, but charming fella, who could easily put both my father and me through a wall if he chose to. I couldn't remember his name at first but while we were recording out first ever episode, (Grover Cleveland) I look over at the man behind the 1s and 2s and remembered that our pal, Chris Covert had referred to the sound guy by his nickname earlier. So, I asked him "what do you think Big Kahuna?" and he hasn't stopped talking since (we love you Christian).

This "book idea" was now a successful podcast. We used money from the podcast's Patreon to fund my first comedy special "Escape from Jacksonville". With a few mega viral clips, I can honestly say it changed my life and my comedy career...

To grow the podcast, we used Mike Harrington's idea taking our craziest episode topics and make them into 90 second clips for Instagram. We then brought in the great Rebecca Kaplan and she edited them into complete magic.

So, Christmas Eve 2023, when I got home from the hospital... I hugged my family, enjoyed Christmas, took a few Tylenol PMs and then set about posting the three Instagram Reels on my page. They took off at a rate I still cannot fathom... not bad for a joke writer from Jersey.

Then we started to notice the follows; my comedy friends enjoyed the content, my navy buddies were all thrilled to see it and then woah did we get noticed... Celebrity accounts, NFL athletes, world famous Comedians and podcasters, all started to follow my account. Which yet again, I took as "proof of concept" we were doing something cool.

To keep the content moving for our newfound audience, I started banging out more scripts. 90 seconds is a long time if you are in a chokehold, but it is rather brief to try and explain the Lincoln Assassination Conspiracy in... but we found ways to make it work. Harrington would film and produce the clips with me at Gas Digital in NYC, Becca would edit masterpieces on the green screen, and I'd find a way to quickly tell the weird stories in the same amount of time as an elevator ride. I asked my girlfriend, Karlie, to help me with some graphic designs and took advice from my father for more "losers" deserving of some attention.

Soon, I realized that I had way more scripts and stories ready to be filmed than I thought and that's when it all clicked...by creating a podcast as avoidance of writing a book, I had now accidentally tricked myself into... writing a book.

So, the idea for a book, turned into a podcast, which turned into Instagram Reels, that turned finally...almost 6 years later... into a book.

If you made it this far, it means a lot. I never thought I'd be here either, but it feels nice to take over a decade of dick jokes, bad puns, and history anecdotes and turn it into this...

CONTENTS

Preface

"It's just a book...how hard can it be to read?"...

Well, the author is a moron (I can say that since I'm the moron who is writing this).

Each story from this book is essentially its own chapter. Sometimes a few details might cross over from story to story but that is just coincidence and ultimately, some people are just larger than life (like TEDDY MF'N ROOSEVELT).

Skip around and enjoy whatever story grabs your attention at any given moment. Some of you will be reading this while in the bathroom...which is perfectly acceptable and encouraged.

Each story should take about two minutes or less to read and maybe add another 15-30 seconds to enjoy Karlie's fantastic illustrations. It's designed so you can pick up where you left off, jump around haphazardly or whatever you'd like. After all, you bought it... so it's yours now and I'm not about to tell you what to do with your property and risk getting in trouble with "TEDDY MF'N ROOSEVELT" from beyond the grave.

Attached at the end of the book are something we are calling "Shop Notes". Larry Burke aka my DILF of a dad has been on this rollercoaster with me the whole way so he has included some notes (as any retired shop teacher would) to give better context to the madness of "American Loser"

When you find yourself done with a story you enjoyed, jump to the back to see what notes Larry Burke set aside for you.

OR

Read the notes first and then decide if you'd like to read the story based on the notes...It is entirely up to you. We wouldn't tell you what to do...lest we risk the wrath of

TEDDY MF'N ROOSEVELT!

Enjoy the book!

HISTORY ISN'T BORING, YOUR TEACHER WAS

Written by KP Burke

CHAPTER 1 - J. EDGAR HOOVER'S SEX TAPE

1. J. EDGAR HOOVER'S SEX TAPE

H ey, there's no such thing as the Deep State, and there's certainly not sex tapes of presidents that were being used against them by people in power. In terms of a life of public service J. Edgar Hoover served almost 50 years as the head of the FBI. Hoover was appointed by Calvin Coolidge and would go on to serve under eight more Presidents. There were times throughout his tenure that people wondered who's really running the country, the President or J Edgar. After the 1936 Olympics, Hoover had his men start a surveillance protocol on a suspected Nazi spy, a sexy Danish reporter named Inga Arvad. While they never found any evidence of her supporting Hitler or even working as a spy, they did find something that would come in handy years later. Inga had been romantically linked to a handsome American naval officer and Hoover kept audio tapes of one of their steamy hotel room encounters. Even though it gave him no evidence, it proved uniquely useful when President Eisenhower left office and his replacement was a brash, young, idealistic, new president named John F. Kennedy. JFK immediately began clashing with the heads of various intelligence community, until Hoover met with the new President and let him know that he had a sex tape of him and Inga Arvad during a pre-WWII investigation. Kind of funny that Hoover seemed to get whatever he wanted during the Kennedy years after that. All it seemed to take was a sex tape. But guys, don't worry about that. Those are just conspiracy theories.

CHAPTER 2 - PHILLY MOB WAR

2. PHILLY MOB WAR

W ell, they blew up the chicken man in Philly last night, and they blew up his house too. That's Bruce Springsteen singing about an event during the brutal Philly mob war of the 1980s. Since 1959, Angelo Bruno had peacefully run the Philly mafia and was known as the Gentle Don. One of the only guys who got in trouble with Bruno was Nicodemo Scarfa A-K-A "little Nicky"; who he banished to Atlantic City. In 1980, the "Gentle Don" was executed with a shotgun blast to the back of his head, ending his peaceful reign and starting a war that would kill at least 20 mobsters in just the next four years. Philip "The Chicken Man" Testa, was now in charge, but as Springsteen told us, his rivals used nail bombs to "blow him up and his house too". This made little Nicky Scarfo, the new boss, alongside his godson, the son of the chicken man, Salvatore Testa. Salvatore Testa inherited his father's house, loan sharking business and a dive bar without a liquor license in Atlantic City called Le Bistro. He was able to make a nice profit though, by selling the property to a real estate developer from Queens named Donald Trump, who turned the building into Trump Plaza and got away with paying about only a third of what the property would have been worth. Testa would be murdered in New Jersey a few years later in 1984, due to jealousy from Little Nicky, his own godfather. And you thought Chase Utley played dirty. Little Nicky would eventually die in prison in 2017. As for Philly, it's still wild.

CHAPTER 3 - AMERICA'S FIRST EMPEROR

3. AMERICA'S FIRST EMPEROR

If you thought the homeless were running San Francisco now, did you know one of them was once Emperor of America? Meet Norton, America's Emperor. Norton was a Jewish fella from England who arrived in San Francisco as a businessman. He did well for himself until 1852, when he made a bold move to try and corner the market on rice during trade bans, which blew up in his face. It broke him financially and mentally. So, he did the only thing a "straight white male" can do, write a manifesto. At the end of it, he declared himself Emperor of the United States. As a joke, a San Francisco newspaper ran the manifesto, and there you have it, America has a self-proclaimed Emperor, his name is Norton, and he lives in a boarding house. Less than a month into his reign, he put out a proclamation where he abolished Congress on behalf of the American people. After that, he abolished the two-party system and ordered General Winfield Scott to use suitable force to clear the halls of Congress. Norton wore a blue uniform of a Union General with gold epaulettes and a rusty battle saber. He ate at free lunch counters with stray dogs and never paid to take the ferry as part of his executive privilege. Soon, he began printing his own currency with his face on it AND on the 1870 census, Norton listed his occupation as "Emperor". The emperor also wrote letters to Queen Victoria of England, explained to her why a marriage to him would help strengthen the relationship between England and America. I mean, look how well worked out for Meghan Markle.

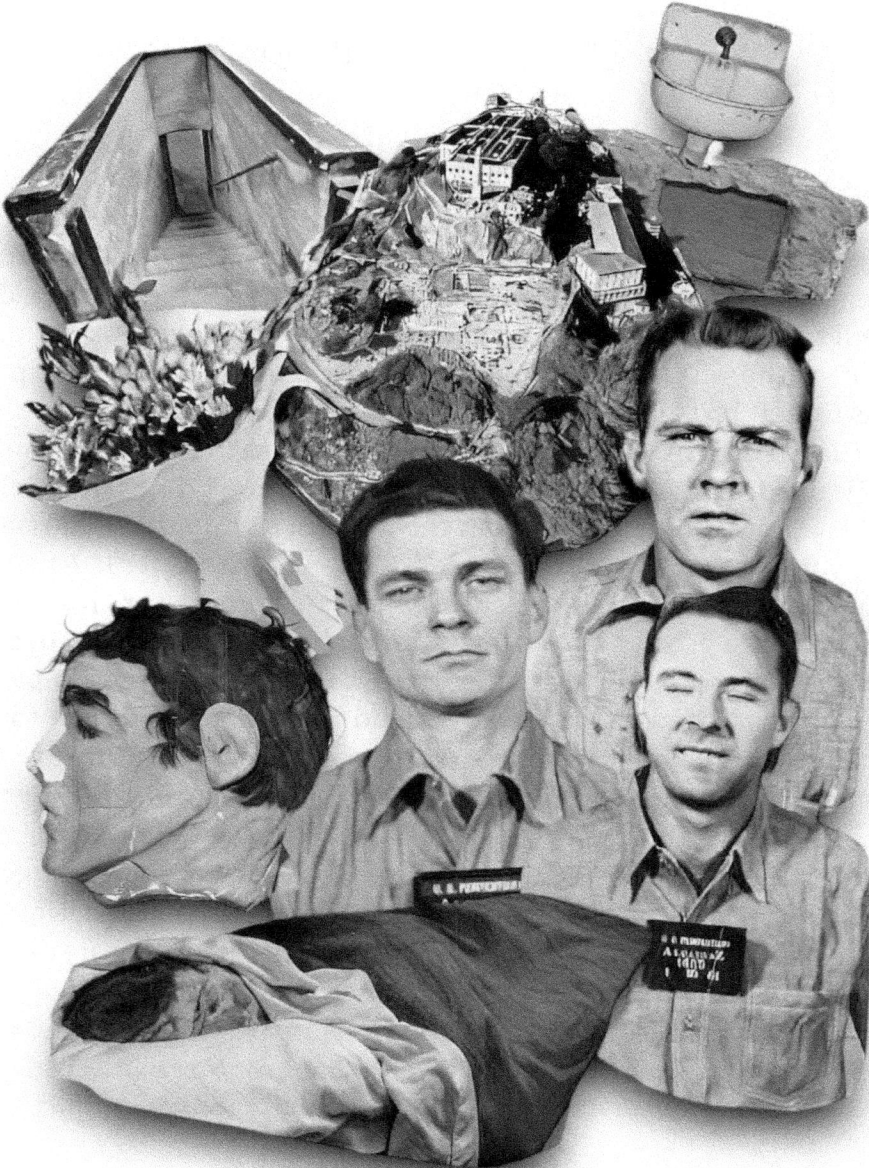

CHAPTER 4 - THE ALCATRAZ ESCAPE

4. THE ALCATRAZ ESCAPE

Alcatraz, the Rock. Nobody escapes, or did this guy? By housing names like Machine Gun Kelly (not that one) and Al Capone, Alcatraz had a reputation as being impossible to escape from with the rough water surrounding the prison island out in San Francisco Bay. However, there is one case in 1962 that even the FBI hasn't solved. And that's the story of Frank Morris and the Anglin brothers. Frank Morris, a lifelong criminal with a dangerously high IQ, had already escaped several prisons before...but Alcatraz was inescapable, or so they thought. He worked quietly together with the Anglin brothers for six months by digging with old saw blades, making a MacGyver like drill out of a vacuum cleaner, covering up the noise with an accordion (not a joke) and using homemade life preservers...oh and the best part of it all, arts and crafts baby! Morris and the boys made papier mache heads with hair and all to make it look that they were sleeping while the guards did "count" every night. On June 11, 1962, Frank and the boys escaped from Alcatraz. The next morning, the FBI launched a massive manhunt and believed the three men had drowned in the bay, but no bodies ever washed up on shore. The case was never solved, but sightings of the three men went on for years afterwards. The best story being that the Anglin brother's mother received anonymous flowers on Mother's Day for the rest of her life and spotted at her funeral were two very tall and unusual women with heavy makeup and large coats on. Did Frank and the boys make it?

CHAPTER 5 - "NAZI" SUMMER CAMP IN LONG ISLAND?

5. "NAZI" SUMMER CAMP IN LONG ISLAND?

Hitler youth one of the most unsettling parts of the Nazi legacy. It must have been terrifying to see young boys and girls supporting Hitler in Germany and... Long Island? The 1930s were crazy time. Nobody knew what to make of that dictator with the funny mustache over in Germany. If only we had seen just how far reaching his plans were... the Nazi Party wanted the United States and its large German population to have a positive view of Hitler. So, what a better way to get into the hearts of the American youth than with summer vacations?! Welcome to Camp Siegfried in Yaphank, Long Island, a summer camp ran by the German American Bund AKA a Nazi funded camp for kids. It had archery, hiking, canoeing, other German kids and being told you are part of the master race?! Sounds like fun, summer camp, pool parties...lots of pictures of Adolf Hitler, (like lots of them) but hey, there's Oktoberfest and good beer and Nazi flags... and lots of Taylor Swift looking chicks trying to breed more Aryan children... In a very eerie testimony during investigations into the camp, one camper was asked how he was taught to salute the American flag. He responded with a perfect Nazi (aka Bellamy) salute. And when asked, "is this the American salute?" ... the camper morbidly said, "it will be". By the time the US was at war with Hitler's Nazi Germany, the camp was shut down by the US Government. Prior to that, all activities have been protected by the First Amendment.

HARRY THAW KILLS STANFORD WHITE IN JEALOUS RAGE OVER ACTRESS WIFE

CHAPTER 6 - THE EPSTEIN BEFORE EPSTEIN

6. THE EPSTEIN BEFORE EPSTEIN

Stanford White... during his life he was a beloved New York architect who designed several buildings, including the iconic Washington Square Arch. But enough about scenes from Ghostbusters. In 1906, Stanford White was approached by a man who took out a gun and said, "you've ruined my wife" and pulled the trigger. Total tragedy. Until it was revealed that Stanford White was secretly one of the worst people in human history. It seems that once he got invited into high society life, Stanford White's demon started to come out. His apartment on 24th Street in Manhattan was revealed to have one room that was painted entirely green with a red velvet swing hanging in the middle of it. That is where he would creepily groom underage girls for his own sordid affairs. Crazy behaviors for a guy commissioned directly by the Vanderbilts?! White used his power and prestige to carry out affairs with young girls, the most famous of which was Evelyn Nesbit, a beautiful model and actress who had been one of White's victims when she was just 16 and White was 48! Years later, Nesbit would marry railroad millionaire Harry Kendall Thaw, who couldn't believe the horrible story his wife told him about her former "friend". His gunshot rang out and Stanford White died inside of a theatre he helped design (Madison Square Theater). The ensuing court case was dubbed the Trial of the Century, with Thaw getting off on account of insanity. According to Mark Twain, who hated Stanford, everyone knew about White, but nothing was ever done. Many of Stanford White's buildings are still standing to this day.

CHAPTER 7 - NAVY SEAL IMPRISONED

7. NAVY SEAL IMPRISONED?

War hero nicknamed "demolition Dick" created Seal Team Six and then later got thrown in prison?! Richard Marcinko tried to join the marines, but they rejected him for not having a high school diploma. Instead, he joined the Navy and began one of the wildest careers in military history. Starting as an enlisted radio man, Marcinko would become an officer and join Seal Team 2 seeing intense combat in Vietnam. After the Iran hostage crisis, it was decided that the Navy needed a full-time counter terrorist unit, and they named Demo Dick as the units first commander. Demo Dick would handpick most of his own men to ensure he had enough chaotic cowboys for his new mission and named them Seal Team Six... even though there were only two Seal teams at the time, Marcinko wanted the Soviet Union to think we had six teams of ass kicking Cowboys from hell ready to respond on a moment's notice. After leaving the team, he began his infamous work with "Red Cell" where he was tasked directly by a Vice Admiral to test the Navy's vulnerability to terrorism. Demo Dick showcased some major concerns for base security when the team of former Seals were able to infiltrate bases, plant bombs near Air Force One, take over a submarine, and kidnap high ranking officers. Red Cell eventually humiliated enough people that Demo Dick had a target on his head, and although he claimed it was a witch hunt, he was sent to 21 months in prison on a kickback trial. When asked about his time in prison, demo Dick called it his "easiest deployment".

CHAPTER 8 - WHO KILLED EDGAR ALLAN POE?

8. WHO KILLED EDGAR ALLAN POE?

The name Edgar Allan Poe conjures up images of horror, mystery and hot goth girls. His legacy is that of a celebrated author, but a tortured soul. Alcoholism, opium use, and mental illness are all part of his legacy. But what if our idea of Poe as a moody, alcoholic, head case is largely taken from his obituary that was written by a guy who straight up hated him?! Poe is one of America's literary icons. He was a soldier, widower, writer, poet, editor and one of America's first ever literary critics. His tales of murder and the Macabre made him a celebrated name, but his life was plagued by tragedy, which explains the dark themes found in all his work. Poe was also a proud Bostonian, even though Baltimore claims his legacy and named their football team after his most popular work, "The Raven". Poe always referred to himself as a Bostonian. Baltimore claims Poe's legacy, but it also claimed his life. Much like Omar from The Wire, Poe found himself dropped on the streets of Charm City. The author was found on October 3rd, 1849, looking disheveled and in need of immediate assistance. He would die a few days later. Many details of his death remain a mystery to this day, but one thing is for sure... Ray Lewis didn't see shit! Poe's obituary, which was published nationwide and written by a man named Ludwig, cast Poe as a lunatic, drug addicted, drunk that nobody was going to miss. Ludwig was later found out to be Rufus Wilmot Griswold, one of pose's biggest rivals and worst enemies. Imagine having your obituary written by somebody that couldn't stand you.

CHAPTER 9 - NYC'S MOST CORRUPT MAYOR?

9. NYC'S MOST CORRUPT MAYOR?

New Yorkers always seem to complain about their mayor, but nobody takes the cake quite like the corrupt brain of Fernando Wood. New York City is built on corruption and no political machine was better than the infamous Tammany Hall, they ran the city like Tony Soprano ran Jersey. Power is running for office; real power is running someone for office. Enter Fernando Wood, the man told by the "powers at be" that he was going to be the first Tammany Hall Mayor of New York City. At times, he was considered the model Mayor, helping to modernize the city, spending money on infrastructure, and moving along the plans for Central Park. But that was his first term. His second term, he barely won re-election, and that's only because he personally ordered the cops off duty and let his gang "The Dead Rabbits" (yes, those dead rabbits) intimidate voters and steal ballot boxes. The wildest part of his time as Mayor was in 1857 when he started the New York City Police riot. To crack down on corruption, New York State took away Woods control of the city's police, they created the Metropolitan Police and ordered Wood to disband his municipal police. Wood was ordered to be arrested, and a full-on brawl between the two police departments would take place in front of city hall for almost an hour, just like in Batman! Wood was eventually arrested and sent to prison for his crimes. Just kidding! He was out that night, ran for mayor again and won. So maybe it's time to cut some other Mayors slack.

CHAPTER 10 - THE STORY OF CINCO DE MAYO

10. THE STORY OF CINCO DE MAYO

Margaritas all around Muchachos. It's time to celebrate Cinco de Mayo, which is, of course Mexican Independence Day, right? Wrong! Salma Hayek's birthday. Well, that is worth celebrating, but not on May 5th. Cinco de Mayo is the yearly celebration of the Mexican victory over the Second French Empire at the Battle of Puebla in 1862. Why was that so important? Well, after the Mexican American War, territory south of the new US borders was sort of up for grabs. A civil war in Mexico nearly bankrupted the entire nation, and the Mexican president, Benito Juarez told England, Spain and France, he wasn't paying back on the loans they took out. France, under the rule of Napoleon the Third, sent troops over to invade Mexico. The Battle of Puebla would take place on, you guessed it... May 5th, 1862. The Mexican troops (outnumbered two to one) managed to defeat the much better equipped French army. The Mexican resistance proved stronger than expected, and some historians credit this Mexican victory with helping to prevent France from aiding the Confederacy during America's Civil War. The victory was short lived, however, and a year later, the French had taken over Mexico City and installed an Austrian monarch named Maximilian as emperor, at least until it all went down in flames. Maximilian was executed via firing squad and Mexican president Juarez declared May 5th, the date of the victory at Puebla as a national holiday, saying, "I don't always defeat the French army, but when I do, I drink Dos Equis".

CHAPTER 11 - WILD PRESIDENT'S DAUGHTER

11. WILD PRESIDENT'S DAUGHTER

Teddy Roosevelt could do a lot of things. He could take San Juan Hill and give a speech with a bullet lodged in his chest, but even the mighty TR struggled with man's greatest foe, his own teenage daughter. If you thought Hunter Biden and the Bush twins were wild, wait till you hear about Alice Roosevelt. Alice was the oldest child of Teddy Roosevelt. Her mother died two days after her birth, and she was raised in Manhattan by her aunt. By the time Teddy became president in 1901, Alice was 17 and a pop culture icon. The outspoken beauty and fashionista enjoyed the nightlife, smoked cigarettes in public, drove in cars with boys, and kept a pet snake in the White House. At times, her life was wilder than a Britney Spears TikTok. Alice would constantly burst into Teddy's office to give her opinion. When someone asked TR if there was anything he could do to limit her interruptions, he said, "I can either run the country or I can attend to Alice, but I cannot possibly do both". When it was time for her family to leave the White House, Alice burned a Voodoo doll of the new First Lady (Nellie Taft), leading to her being banned from the White House by the next two administrations. Naturally, Alice's wedding was a wild affair. The bride showed up in a blue dress and cut her own wedding cake with a sword. Alice never allowed a dull moment, as even in her older years, she was nearly banned from the White House a third time after making too many jokes about the Kennedy's. She would die at age 96, and is immortalized by her quote, "If you can't say anything nice about someone, come sit here next to me".

CHAPTER 12 - DID THIS ANARCHIST CHANGE AMERICA?

12. DID THIS ANARCHIST
CHANGE AMERICA?

If you ever felt like one person can make a difference in America, let me tell you about Leon Czolgosz. He was a Polish fellow from Detroit Rock City, who changed the face of America forever with one pull of a trigger, but not in the way he had hoped. Leon Czolgosz was born in Detroit in 1873 and after the panic of 1893 closed the mill he was employed by, Leon began to have major concerns over economic injustices. He found himself hanging out with socialist anarchists and other types you can find in a hipster coffee shop. The socially awkward Leon became radicalized and decided to take matters into his own hands. So... he picked his target, the President of the United States, William McKinley. While McKinley was greeting the public, Leon shot him twice in the abdomen. Around this time, an African American fella named James Parker went full "Equalizer" on Leon, knocking the gun out of his hand, then hitting him so hard he spun like a cartoon, broke his nose and knocked out several of the assassin's teeth. The UFC style K-O was so brutal that even the wounded president said out loud "go easy on him boys". McKinley would die eight days later, and Leon would plead guilty and be sentenced to death by the electric chair. If Leon's goal was anarchy, he accomplished that because by killing President Mckinley, we swore in his Vice President, and that's how America wound up with President Teddy Mother F**king Roosevelt.

CHAPTER 13 - NASA AND THE OCCULT LINKED?

13. NASA AND THE OCCULT LINKED?

We've all heard of sex, drugs and rock and roll, but what about sex, drugs and rocket science? Meet Jack Parsons, the man who helped launch the US space program, operate a sex cult and accidentally started a religion. Jack Parsons liked reading about strange things and blowing stuff up. He was fascinated by the occult and as a teenager, summoned the Devil, which may or may not have worked. Parsons would become a brilliant chemist and rocket scientist but in 1939, Jack and his wife were taken to the Church of Thelema in Hollywood, and Jack's obsession with the occult deepened. He caught the eye of Aleister Crowley and began to combine the occults "sex magick" with his understanding of quantum physics and more importantly, jet propulsion. Parsons was addicted to several drugs and regularly took part in black magic, but his rocketry work was good enough that the government turned a blind eye to his screwball behavior. Parsons would then meet L. Ron Hubbard (yes, that one), smart enough to help create the modern space shuttle, but for some reason, he was not smart enough to not let L. Ron Hubbard run off with his wife down to Florida with his life savings. L. Ron and Parson's wife Sara would go on to create Dianetics and founded the Church of Scientology. After being bankrupted and blacklisted, Parsons would die in 1952 from mysterious explosion in his home laboratory. We eventually did put a man on the moon, but it took a black magic practicing sex addict on drugs to help us pull it off.

CHAPTER 14 - AMERICA'S FIRST "INFLUENCER"?

14. AMERICA'S FIRST "INFLUENCER"?

W hat's the difference between propaganda and public relations? Well, let's ask Edward Bernays. To put it simply, Edward Bernays was the original "influencer". He was related to Sigmund Freud and applied his cousin's research thoroughly while working for the U.S. Government during WWI in what he called "psychological warfare". After the war, he was hired by Beech Nut Packing Company to help them "sell more bacon". Bernays was able to develop the idea that breakfast was the most important meal of the day, and it was un-American to have it without bacon. Bernays was also hired by Lucky Strike to help get women to start smoking more. He created propaganda showing only thin and attractive women smoking and appealed to feminists by calling cigarettes "torches of freedom". Take that patriarchy... now all the ladies can give themselves cancer too! Eventually, Bernays began working for the UFC (no, not that one). The United Fruit Company wanted to sell more bananas in the US, and it worked until Guatemala's President's reforms began affecting sales. Bernays then started up a propaganda effort showing Guatemala in grave danger from communism, which led to the CIA overthrowing their government in 1954..."Banana Republic" Get it? Bernays would die in 1995. By then, the UFC was now Chiquita, Feminists were smoking Virginia slims, and propaganda was now known as "public relations". Bernays was survived by his loving family, including his grandnephew Marc Randolph, the co- founder of... yeah, Netflix.

CHAPTER 15 - NATIVE AMERICAN CURSE ON PRESIDENCY

15. NATIVE AMERICAN CURSE ON PRESIDENCY

I s it possible that an old Native American holy man put a fatal curse in the office of the presidency in 1840? William Henry Harrison was elected president of the United States, his nickname was "Old Tippecanoe" after a battle he had fought against a legendary group of Native Americans under Tecumseh. Tecumseh's brother was a holy man, and the story goes that he cursed the future president. Nothing really came of it until 1840, when Harrison was sworn in as president. He would die in office just a few months later of pneumonia. This was the start of what became known is the "Curse of Tippecanoe". When a president is elected in a year that ends in a zero, strange and terrible things seem to happen to that man. For example, elected in 1840, William Henry Harrison dies in office. Elected in 1860, Abraham Lincoln assassinated in office. Elected in 1880, James A Garfield assassinated in office. Elected in 1900, William McKinley assassinated in office. In 1920, Warren G Harding dies in office (foul play still suspected). From an election in 1940, FDR dies in office (died 1945). In 1960, John F Kennedy is assassinated (COUGH by the CIA). Elected in 1980, Ronald Reagan barely survives an assassination attempt. Elected in 2000, George W Bush also luckily survives after a live grenade thrown at him does not detonate. Which leads us to the year 2020... Joe Biden was elected and as of the time of writing (Book Published in 2024) ... is still technically President but is it possible that Tecumseh and his brother were responsible for that debate performance?

CHAPTER 16 - DOLLEY SAVES GEORGE WASHINGTON

16. DOLLEY MADISON SAVES GEORGE WASHINGTON

This Painting of George Washington is Iconic, but it was almost burned and lost forever until it was saved at the last minute by a sexy party girl and First Lady named Dolley Madison. Long before England and America had our special relationship, there was plenty of hostility left over from the whole "revolution" thing. This leads us to the largely skipped over War of 1812. It went bad for us early on, so bad that in 1814, the British took over D.C., they burned federal buildings, torched the Presidential Mansion, AKA the White House, shit in Nancy Pelosi's desk, and burned the Capitol building. Try that one on Q-anon! President James Madison decided it was time for him and his Danny DeVito looking ass to evacuate D.C. This included his sexy wife, Dolley, who was the coolest first lady of all time. She was also a huge fan of George Washington and with just minutes to spare before the British could capture the "Celebrity First Lady", Dolley sent her trusted servant Paul Jennings (a black dude), to save the famous portrait of General Washington. The British surely would have burned it, but thanks to Dolley, it was saved. And then something happened... The Americans ate their vitamins, said their prayers and went full hulkamania. So, thanks to Dolley (and Paul's heroics) the Americans started kicking some ass again. We wrote the Star-Spangled Banner and won a bloody battle down in New Orleans (that technically happened after the war was over, but it still counts DAMMIT!).

CHAPTER 17 - DEVIL DAN SICKLES

17. DEVIL DAN SICKLES

Nobody in American politics has a story quite like "Devil" Dan Sickles. It involves hookers, murder, Gettysburg and the Queen of Spain. Sickles was a Tammany Hall Democrat, elected to the Senate in 1856. He had a smoking hot wife but also had a penchant for hanging out with prostitutes. In fact, he got in trouble for introducing a hooker to Queen Victoria under the alias of one of his political enemies. To put that in modern context, imagine if Trump brought Stormy Daniels to meet the Queen and introduced her as "Hillary Clinton". Sickles wife was having an affair of her own, with District Attorney Phillip Barton Key, the son of Francis Scott Key (the guy who wrote the star-spangled banner). Sickles learned of the affair, then shot and killed his wife's lover within view of the White House. He pled "temporary insanity", which had never been tried in America before and it worked. Sickles would seek to rehab his public image during the Civil War and at the Battle of Gettysburg. He would go "FULL LEGEND" having disobeyed orders; Sickles got his leg blown off by a cannon but kept smoking a cigar from his hospital stretcher. This would win him a visit from President Abe Lincoln himself AND his leg would be put on display in a museum (it's still there). Not only did Sickles survive losing a leg, but he would also regularly take people to visit it on display at a museum years after the battle. After the war he served as minister to Spain and quickly began banging Isabella the Second, the Queen of Spain. Sickles would die at the age of 94 in Manhattan and is the only Major General to NOT have a statue at Gettysburg because he embezzled the money.... true story.

CHAPTER 18 - WIZARD OF OUNCES?

18. THE WIZARD OF OUNCES?

The Wizard of Oz, a classic film was based on a book, which was based on political propaganda? In the late 1800s a major issue in America was "bi-metallism" AKA the argument between the Gold Standard VS "Free Silver". The most famous Champion of Free Silver was William Jennings Bryan, a guy who would run for President as many times as the Buffalo Bills have lost super bowls. Bryan came to fame in 1896 as the Democratic Presidential nominee and would run against William McKinley, who believed in the Gold Standard. But what does this have to do with the Wizard of Oz? Well, L. Frank Baum the eventual author of the Wizard of Oz, campaigned for McKinley, which led some historians to believe that the "Wizard of Oz" is a political satire. Dorothy comes from Kansas, she's everything that is good and honest about America but is lost thanks to a twister, which is a metaphor for the struggling economy. In the movie version, her slippers are red but, in the book, they are made of silver, which is super important. She must follow the "yellow brick road" ...aka the Gold Standard to get to Emerald City aka paper currency...where the power of OZ can get her back home. OZ, which is the abbreviation for ounces, which is what we measure gold in.... yup. Along the way, she will meet a scarecrow aka Farmers, a tin woodsman, aka Factory workers and that cowardly lion also known as William Jennings Bryan. Lions and Tigers and Politicians oh my!

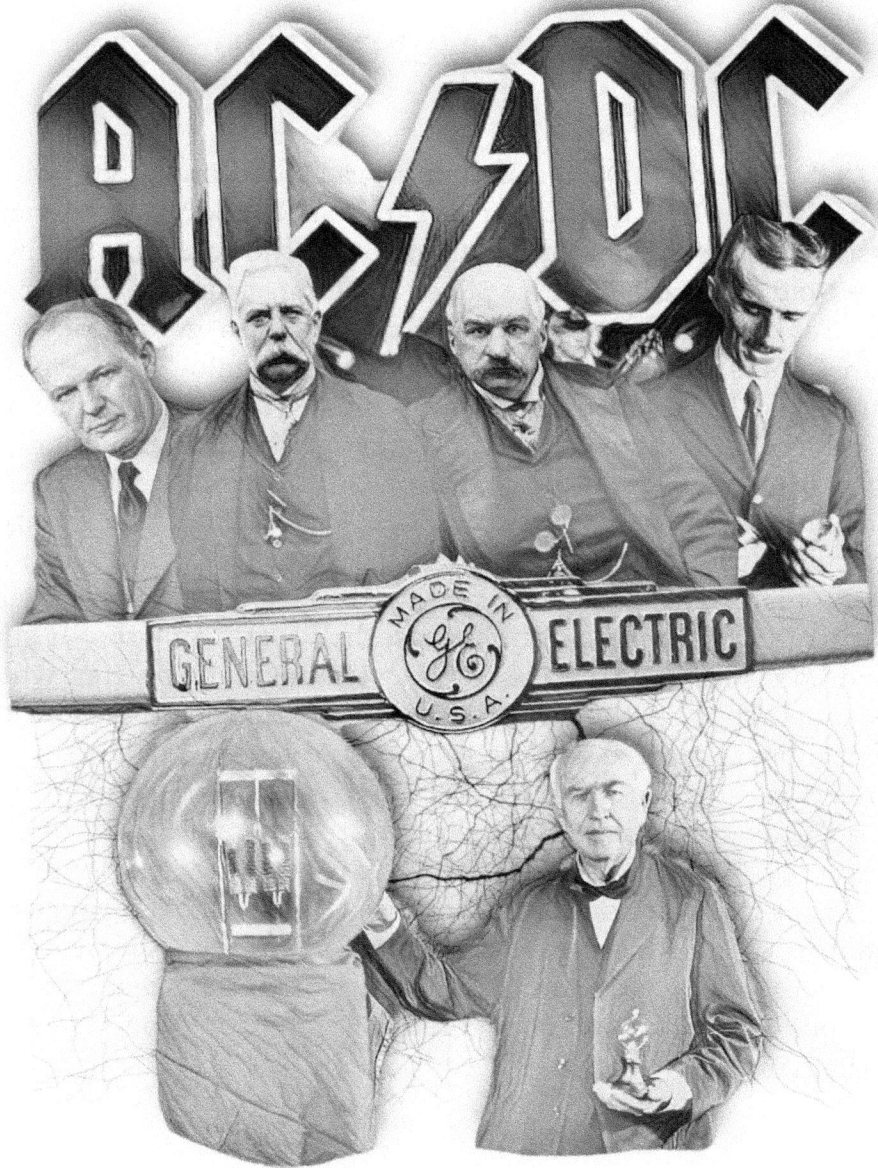

CHAPTER 19 - WAR OF THE CURRENTS

19. THE WAR OF CURRENTS

A C/DC makes me think of "back in black" but the battle between AC AND DC was full of legitimate dirty deeds done dirt cheap. The "War of the Currents" was waged largely between two men, Thomas Edison and his former employee, a quirky Serbian immigrant named Nikola Tesla. Tesla was a proponent of Alternating Current, but Edison had already invested heavily in his Direct Current system and had major money backers to answer to. Between this clash of ideologies AND a joke that got "lost in translation", Tesla stormed out and George Westinghouse (Edison's chief rival) jumped at the chance to buy Tesla's AC patents. After a long and dirty propaganda effort, complete with lawsuits, patent stealing, corporate takeovers and the invention of the electric chair (check out that chapter if you haven't) the current war was over and Edison had won, except... he didn't. Against his wishes, "The EDISON GENERAL ELECTRIC COMPANY" would wind up adopting alternating current (validating his rival Tesla) and after mergers with the likes of JP Morgan...Edison not only lost direct current, but his company dropped his name as well.... becoming General Electric aka....GE. As for Tesla...he died penniless, but his remaining work was seized by the FBI and given for analysis to an MIT Scientist named...John G Trump...whose nephew is.... yeah, him...wild.

CHAPTER 20 - THE KINDER FORM OF CAPITAL PUNISHMENT

20. THE KINDER FORM OF
CAPITAL PUNISHMENT

Did you know the Electric Chair was once considered the more humane form of execution? The traditional form of capital punishment in America was death by hanging but that was getting a little too gruesome post-Civil War. Enter Alfred P Southwick, a dentist who used one of his old dental chairs to invent the electric chair.... that's right a dentist...keep brushing kids. How can we safely utilize electricity? Should we go with Direct Current, as championed by Thomas Edison...or Alternating Current, the idea of one of Edison's former employees...Nikola Tesla? Alternating Current vs Direct Current, AC vs DC...AC/DC ...not that one but don't worry we're still on a highway to hell here. To show how dangerous his rival's Alternating current was, Edison would utilize underhanded means to have AC used for the execution of death row inmate William Kemmler on August 6th, 1890. After the first blast was sent through Kemmler, the prisoner was still alive! After doubling the voltage, Kemmler finally did die but not before smoke came off his body and the room started to smell like...well you get the picture. Despite the "botched" first attempt, within 20 years the electric chair was now mainstream and even had "famous" chairs like New York's "Old Sparky", New Jersey's "Old Smokey", Louisiana's "Gruesome Gertie" and Alabama's infamous "Yellow Mama".

CHAPTER 21 - THE 20TH PRESIDENT'S ASSASSIN

21. THE 20TH PRESIDENT'S ASSASSIN

Everyone knows about Lincoln and JFK, but Poor James A. Garfield really is the Jan Brady of assassinated Presidents. James A Garfield was the 20th President of the United States until.... he was shot on July 2nd, 1881; except he didn't die....at least not right away. He died three months later from infection in Long Branch, New Jersey....and you thought Snooki had a rough summer down the shore. Who shot the President? Well, it was a guy that campaigned for him...Meet Charles J. Guiteau aka Manson before Manson. Charles was a narcissistic, schizophrenic lawyer that got into politics after being kicked out of a sex cult (the cult now makes silverware but that is a story for another time). Guiteau had convinced himself that he helped Garfield win the Presidency but when the President and the rest of D.C. ignored the awkward creepy Guiteau. He went out and bought a gun telling the store clerk it needed "ivory handles so it would look good in a museum one day". Guiteau waited in the ladies' room at the Baltimore Potomac Railroad Station and then shot the President twice. President Garfield would die months later, September 19th 1881...a Monday.... which explains why Garfield hates Mondays. As for Guiteau, he would act as his own attorney, be found guilty and sentenced to death but not before he danced his way to the gallows and read a poem he wrote as his final words. His gun was somehow lost, BUT part of his brain was preserved in a jar and can be found in the Mutter Museum in Philadelphia. I'm not kidding.

CHAPTER 22 - THE JERSEY DEVIL

22. THE JERSEY DEVIL

B enjamin Franklin once roasted a rival so hard...that the NHL named a team after it? Franklin has been credited as arguably the most important "founding father" who gained fame and wealth thanks to his writing career, most notably his annual " Poor Richards Almanack". Franklin's rival publication was the "American Almanack" which had been started by Daniel Leeds. Leeds lived in the Pine Barrens near modern day Atlantic City, New Jersey. He studied mysticism and magic, which got him kicked out of the Quaker community and publicly called "the devil". Daniel Leeds died in 1720. Titan Leeds, Daniel's son continued publishing his family's yearly Almanac until a joke by Benjamin Franklin launched the Leeds Family into folklore forever. Franklin used his almanac's first edition in 1732 to predict that Titan would die on October 17th, 1733. When that date came to pass and Titan Leeds was still alive, Franklin posted an obituary jokingly claiming that Titan had died. Titan publicly called Franklin a "fool" and "liar", which led to Franklin suggesting that Titan had indeed died but was now writing his criticism as a "ghost". Titan would die 5 years later but Franklin's joke, combined with Daniel Leeds reputation, led to the story of The Leeds Family Devil...a monster creature with wings and hooves (inspired by the Leeds family coat of arms). This monster is said to haunt the Pine Barrens with many over the centuries claiming to have spotted it. The story of the Jersey Devil became so popular that 248 years after the prank...we named our hockey team...the New Jersey Devils.

CHAPTER 23 - THE LINCOLN CONSPIRACY

23. THE LINCOLN CONSPIRACY

A braham Lincoln is remembered for his tragic death when he was assassinated at Ford's Theatre by John Wilkes Booth. After "whacking" the President, Booth would be killed in gunfight with Union troops...end of story, right? What gets skipped over is Booth's other conspirators, George Azerodt, David Herold, Lewis Powell, and especially Mary Surratt...who holds the distinction of being the first woman executed by the US Government. "Unaliving" Lincoln was part of a larger plot. The conspiracy also involved the killing of Vice President Andrew Johnson and Secretary of State William Seward. Booth tasked Herold (a pharmacist) and Powell (a confederate soldier turned spy) with "whacking" the Secretary of State. Their plan failed, as Seward and his family fought off Powell, who then attempted to escape D.C. after Herold...who was supposed to be his guide, already ran off. Azerodt was tasked with "merking" the VP but instead, got drunk and passed out. Powell was captured while in disguise, Herold surrendered during the showdown with Booth, Atzerodt was in custody and the aforementioned Mary Surratt, was arrested for aiding in the conspiracy that was planned in her boarding house. The unlucky 4 were executed by hanging on July 7th, 1865...with John Wilkes Booth's team having failed on all parts aside from his own, it's no wonder that his last words were, "USELESS, USELESS, USELESS!".

CHAPTER 24 - THE AMERICAN SCOUNDREL

24. THE AMERICAN SCOUNDREL

J ames Wilkinson would fight in the American Revolution and went on to serve under the first four Presidents... sounds like a hero... but instead, he proved to be America's first "Super Villain". Wilkinson embellished his role in the Revolution to get a promotion. Even though George Washington never fully trusted him, Washington found Wilkinson useful when he leaked info about an attempt to have Washington replaced in a conspiracy known as "Conway's Cabal". After the war, Wilkinson would become a paid spy for the Spanish, going by the code name "Agent 13". Wilkinson also undermined the newly formed US Army after not getting a promotion he felt he deserved, even though he was LEGIT SPYING FOR SPAIN! Not only did he never seem to get caught, but he also always found a way to get promoted. Now, as the Governor of the Louisiana territory (AND STILL A SPY), Wilkinson found himself involved in yet another conspiracy. This time, with former VP Aaron Burr and his plan to start his own country! Wilkinson supported Burr's plan until he realized it wasn't going to work, so he ratted Burr out to Thomas Jefferson. Burr was put on trial for treason, Wilkinson cleared the charges, but his reputation was ruined. Until the War of 1812, where he got promoted yet again, DESPITE BEING A SPY FOR SPAIN AND TAKING PART IN TWO MAJOR CONSPIRACIES AGAINST THE U.S.! Everyone knew he was a spy, but no one proved it while Wilkinson was alive. He would die in Mexico City in 1825 and is remembered as the General who "never won a battle yet never lost a court martial".

CHAPTER 25 - THE WHISKEY REBELLION

25. THE WHISKEY REBELLION

America and Whiskey go hand in hand. Whiskey was so important in America that it even had its own rebellion... It's 1791, George Washington is President, and the country has tons of debt from the Revolutionary War... SO Alexander Hamiliton (yes, the guy from the Musical), decides to put a tax on Whiskey being distilled in the United States. Thomas Jefferson was against this, and he was right... the "Whiskey Tax" did not go over so hot. In areas like Western Pennsylvania, distilling Whiskey was common and even used as a currency amongst farmers. This was a tax on those who relied on corn, rye and grain... if nothing else, it was the first tax imposed on a domestic product by the new federal government and it was wildly unpopular. In 1794, a group of over 600 "rebels" in Western PA burned down the Tax Collector's house. President Washington would then lead his US Army himself one more time, on a march out West. His plan worked and the rebels dispersed. Washington handled it like a pro and put down the rebellion without having to fire a single shot. He proved that the federal government could enforce its laws, when necessary BUT he also pardoned the men that were found guilty of treason. Oh, and then...opened his own distillery. True story. A few years later, Thomas Jefferson repealed the tax, and whiskey remains an embodiment of the American Spirit...

LAWRENCE PATRICK "LP" BURKE

SHOP NOTES BY LP

* * *

Chapter 1 - J. Edgar Hoover's Sex Tape

 J. Edgar had a very long list of influential people from all walks of life, not just politicians.

U.S. House of Representatives order an investigation of potential leads of various conspiracies in the JFK assassination. Questionable to how thorough Hoover's FBI carried out that order. Same thing for Bobby Kennedy's assassination.

* * *

Chapter 2 - Philly Mob War

Philadelphia, "The City of Brotherly Love", until you're part of the wrong family.

That went beyond who has the best Philly cheesesteaks. Pat's King of Steaks vs Geno's Steaks.

* * *

Chapter 3 - America's First Emperor

America has been very, very good to me. Where else can an immigrant with a failed business grow up to become Emperor of these United States.

Chapter 4 - The Alcatraz Escape

You can learn a lot of life skills in shop class.

The FBI worked the case for 17 years until 1979, when they turned over the responsibility to the United States Marshals Service.

"Very tall and unusual women with heavy makeup and large coats on" were also spotted at the last pride parade. It was reported they too had spent some time in the San Francisco Bay area.

* * *

Chapter 5 - "Nazi" Summer Camp In Long Island?

Summer camp fun was not just in Long Island. The German American Bund had over 70 regional divisions operating 20 youth and training camps across the country.

On February 20, 1939, the Bund holds a rally in Madison Square Garden that is attended by 20,000 supporters. Hitler invades Poland in September of 1939.

* * *

Chapter 6 - The Epstein Before Epstein

Madison Square Garden 1891, Washington Memorial Arch, New York Herald Building, Madison Square Presbyterian Church are all Stanford White commissions. Private homes including the Vanderbilt's and Astor's were also White designs. Many of Whites works are now National Historic Landmarks.

White is murdered at the Roof Top Supper Club of Madison Square Garden, a facility that White designed.

Chapter 7 - They Put A Navy Seal In Prison?

After commanding Seal Team Six, Demo Dick is called upon to command Red Cell. This newly formed unit was to test the vulnerabilities and security lapses of the U.S. Military bases and U.S. security interests worldwide.

Red Cell is very good at what they were ordered to do and embarrassed too many high-level brass. They were able to break into secure areas, nuclear submarines, Navy ships and even Air Force One. All of this was documented with video used to compile after actions reviews to correct the breaches.

❊ ❊ ❊

Chapter 8 - Who Killed Edgar Allan Poe?

Many theories to what exactly took him out. There is nothing conclusive as to the cause of death. Poe's remains are dug up and moved a couple of times and stone markers misplaced. Are you finally Resting in Peace Edgar? Nevermore.

❊ ❊ ❊

Chapter 9 - New York City's Most Corrupt Mayor?

In 1861, Mayor Wood proposed to New York City Council that the city should secede from the Union and declare itself an independent city - state. This would allow New York to continue its profitable cotton trade with the Confederacy even though the rest of the Union are at war with those guys.

He moves on to higher office and serves 16 years in the House of Representatives and serves as Chairman of the House Committee on Ways and Means. He was married 3 times and had 16 children with wife #2 and #3. No cable TV.

Chapter 10 - The Story Of Cinco De Mayo

The Mexicans opened a can of whoop ass for their French invaders. As few as 2,000 Mexican soldiers with outdated weaponry defeated 6,000 well equipped French soldiers at the Battle of Puebla.

Although it is not a big holiday in Mexico, it was some Californians that really got the Cinco De Mayo party started.

* * *

Chapter 11 - The President's Daughter Did What?

TR's mother dies. Eleven hours later his first wife Alice, also dies two days after giving birth to baby Alice. Teddy is so distraught with this double whammy that he would not allow the name Alice to be mentioned in his presence. It was a too painful reminder of his now deceased wife. Newborn baby Alice is given the nickname "Baby Lee". Teddy never calls his daughter by her correct name. Would that play on a kid's head?

Infant Alice is in the care of TR's sister Anna, known as "Bamie" or Bye until she is two years old. During this time TR leaves the NY State assembly to seek solace in the Bad Lands of North Dakota.

TR remarries and Alice rejoins with her dad and stepmother Edith. Alice and Edith did not see eye to eye on many occasions. Smoking cigarettes was deemed inappropriate for a First Daughter, so Alice went up on the White House roof to smoke.

* * *

Chapter 12 - Did This Anarchist Change America?

Czolgosz becomes interested in and attends various anarchist meetings. The radical newspaper "Free Society" issues warning to other comrades that he is not to be trusted.

The first execution by electric chair takes place at Auburn prison in 1890. Eleven years later Leon is given the same opportunity to have a seat in "Old Sparky" for the assassination of President William McKinley.

After McKinley's death, VP Theodore Roosevelt becomes President. New President TR declares, "When compared with suppression of anarchy, every other question sinks into insignificance".

* * *

Chapter 13 - Nasa And The Occult Linked?

Coincidence or something more sinister?

Jack Parsons and L. Ron Hubbard team up to summon a spirit from another dimension, the sex goddess Babalon. AKA the Scarlet Woman.

Hey Jack, is that a rocket in your pocket or are you just a bird dog for Scarlet?

* * *

Chapter 14 - America's First "Influencer"?

Bernays works on a campaign for Dixie Cup. It was designed to convince American consumers that only disposable cups were sanitary. Imagery of an overflowing cup are linked to subliminal images of genitalia and venereal disease. That's not a pretty picture.

Bacon and eggs are the true all-American breakfast. Ladies light up that cigarette to show their nonconformity and freedom from male oppression. Guatemala isn't the only "banana republic" that Miss Chiquita Banana was heavily influenced by.

Edward Bernays Doctor of Spin. Sorry, I meant to say pioneer to public relations.

Chapter 15 - Native American Curse On Presidency

Don't mess with Native American profits at the casino. Don't mess with "The Prophet", Tenskwatawa, brother of Tecumseh. That was some long-lasting curse.
How come there was never much about Tecumseh in school history books?

Could it be that one man's freedom fighter is another man's terrorist?

❋ ❋ ❋

Chapter 16 - Dolley Madison Saves George Washington

This was no small painting that Dolley rescued. The Gilbert Stuart portrait of Washington measured about 5'x8'. In shop terms, bigger that a full sheet of plywood.

The British burned the Capitol, White House and other buildings in August 1814. It was in large part a retaliation for the Americans looting and burning of the Legislative Assembly and other government buildings in York, now Toronto, Ontario in April 1813. Tit for tat.

Dolley served ice cream at the White House for dinners and receptions, including her husband's second inaugural ball in 1813. Dolley Madison, was a whole lot more than just the ice cream first lady.

❋ ❋ ❋

Chapter 17 - Devil Dan Sickles

At the age of 32, he married his pregnant girlfriend, 15-year- old Teresa Bagioli, the daughter of a close friend.

After murdering Philip Barton Key, Sickles hired Edwin Stanton as his lawyer, who would later become President Lincoln's secretary of war.

At the trial, for the first time ever, a plea of temporary insanity is successfully used, and Sickles is acquitted.

During the Civil War he is given command of the Third Corps by his good friend and fellow womanizer, Major General Joe Hooker. There was a total of 25 Union Corps. Sickles is the only corps commander that did not attend the US Military Academy (West Point). It's not what you know but who you know.

❋ ❋ ❋

Chapter 18 - The Wizard Of Ounces?

A high school teacher named Harry Littlefield connects "The Wizard of Oz" and its author Frank Baum to the late 19th century political movement.

Emerald City, isn't that where them US Greenbacks are printed? Paper money not backed by anything of tangible value. Sounds pretty crypto to me.

❋ ❋ ❋

Chapter 19 - The War Of Currents

A demonstration backed by Edison is held at Columbia College in New York where a 76-pound dog is electrocuted using AC current. This was in part of Edison's propaganda campaign to show how his DC current was safer than Tesla's AC current.

Casualties in the War of the Currents, Edison's team would kill 44 dogs, 6 calves and 2 horses in their quest to discredit alternating current.

No animals were harmed in the making of this book!

❋ ❋ ❋

Chapter 20 - The Kinder Form Of Capital Punishment

Hanging, firing squad or electrocution...we should all have freedom of choice. Pick your poison.

The electric chair is invented by a dentist. "Painless dentistry" soon to follow.

❋ ❋ ❋

Chapter 21 - The 20Th President's Assassin

President Garfield survived for 80 days after being shot, suffering horrendous medical care from doctors untrained in antiseptic methods.

At his trial, the assassin Guiteau stated "I did not kill the President. The doctors did that. I merely shot him." The jury didn't see it that way and Guiteau is hung.

Robert Todd Lincoln, son of Abe Lincoln is present or nearby when three Presidential assassinations take place. He is at his father's deathbed in 1865, he is an eyewitness to Charles Guiteau shooting President Garfield in 1881 and attended the 1901 Pan-American Exposition when President William McKinley was shot by Leon Czolgosz.

❋ ❋ ❋

Chapter 22 - The Jersey Devil

Legend tells us that "Mother Leeds" had twelve children. Upon discovery that she is pregnant once again with number 13, she cursed the unborn child and stated it would be the devil. Mother's love not so much.

Did Ben Franklin know Mother Leeds? Philadelphia to South Jersey Pine Barrens is not that far away.

Chapter 23 - The Lincoln Conspiracy

The initial plan was to kidnap not assassinate President Lincoln and other high-level government officials.

Investigators shorten a very long list of suspects in the conspiracy to ten individuals. Four of the accused are sentenced to hang, four are sentenced to imprisonment (three for life at hard labor, and one for six years). John Wilkes Booth is killed while captured by Federal troops. John Harrison Surratt is later apprehended in Egypt, extradited back to the US and tried. The case results in a hung jury.

*　*　*

Chapter 24 - The American Scoundrel

Theodore Roosevelt described Wilkinson as "In all our history, there is no more despicable character."

Wilkinson alters a letter written to him by Aaron Burr. The altered letter is an attempt to clear Wilkinson of guilt in the conspiracy with Burr to set up a separate country in the Texas territory. When the tampered evidence is discovered, Burr was acquitted. President Jame Madison calls for the court -martial of commanding American General James Wilkinson. Jim W. beats the rap.

The name Benedict Arnold is synonymous with the traitor for selling the plans of West Point to the British. James Wilkinson should be right alongside Benny Arnold for some shenanigans he got away with.

*　*　*

Chapter 25 - The Whiskey Rebellion

The British tried to tax the American colonists with a tax on tea. That ends with a bunch of British tea being dumped in the

Boston Harbor. When the new American government tries to tax whiskey, it leads to a new armed rebellion. Them country folk ain't a gonna stand for that.

Years later the argument distills down to taste great vs. less filling.

AUTHOR KP BURKE AND FAMILY PHOTOS

ABOUT THE AUTHOR

KP Burke is many things. He's a stand-up comedian, a Navy Veteran, an American History junkie and now, an author. Burke considers himself lucky to have had the opportunities in life because of his parents Larry and Sandie Burke, who adopted him at birth in 1987 and raised in Northern New Jersey. Thanks to his parents, KP was able to develop a passion for history from childhood, which was full of trips to battlefields, forts and museums. Early in his youth, the trips to Fort Ticonderoga and Fort William Henry fascinated him endlessly and the first family vacation to Gettysburg pretty much sealed Burke's fate as a "history nerd".

Burke, never an academic, attempted to go to Bergen Community College after high school. He did so well that they suggested he join the military and never come back... He left for the United States Navy in January of 2007 and was stationed aboard the USS Carney as a Hull Maintenance Technician (they told him he'd be a welder/firefighter but all he really did was fix toilets). He would also later serve with the Maritime Security Squadron 10 which would deploy him to Dubai in 2011. Here he would be doing armed security where everyone encouraged him to pursue comedy because he was very funny and could probably get him to turn in his firearms and finally get out of the military.

Burke began performing stand up in March of 2012 and by every conceivable metric... it ruined his life. He immediately caught the eye of Chris Buck, the preeminent comedy writer of Jacksonville, Florida where Burke lived due to the Navy. He was soon working road gigs in the SEC region of the country.

After a breakup, Burke returned home to New Jersey and began working hard at blending his passions of comedy and history between performing in NYC and NJ. He also made his second attempt at higher education at Brookdale Community College where his writing and history professors helped him develop all the skills that led to writing this book.

The "Roastmasters" competitions at "The Stand" in NYC (YouTube KP Burke Roasts for more details) led to Burke's growing reputation as a talented joke writer and afforded him several opportunities to grow such as working with legendary comics like Robert Kelly, Nick DiPaolo, Rich Vos and his comedy hero, Colin Quinn. These events all led to the creation of "American Loser", the podcast Burke created with his father. Burke's first comedy special "Escape from Jacksonville" was released in 2022, featuring several viral clips and solidifying his reputation as one of New Jersey's most talented comics. His second album "The Last Recital" will be released in late 2024.

"AMERICAN LOSER" GUESTS, FRIENDS AND FAMILY